Contents and Glossary

GW01237705

This book will introduce the follo

Adjectives

An **adjective** tells us more about a **noun** (an object, person, event or place).

Tick each **adjective** as you see it describing the dinosaur.

stripy ☐	big ☐	hungry ☐	
purple ☐	spiky ☐	spotty ☐	

Write down some **adjectives** to describe one of your friends.

Adjectives can be placed before a **noun**.

A **tall**, **spotty** dinosaur.

Adjectives can also come after **verbs**, such as 'be' and 'look'.

The dinosaur looks **tall** and **spotty**.

Use some of these **adjectives** to finish these sentences.

small   red   clean
colourful   new

It is a _____ bicycle.

Your jumper looks _____.

Think about your favourite toy. Write three **adjectives** to describe it here.

_____

_____

_____

Well done!

5

Using adjectives

We usually put **adjectives** in the following order: **size**, **age**, **colour**.

That is Rosie's **large**, **new**, **blue** bag.

size	age	colour

Use a **comma** between the adjectives when they come one after another.

Rewrite this note putting the **adjectives** in the correct order. Don't forget to add the commas in the right place.

We took our green small bucket to the beach and used our yellow new spades.

Words that have the same, or similar meaning, are called **synonyms**. They make sentences more interesting.

It was a **good** party.

It was a **wonderful** party.
It was a **fantastic** party.

Circle the **synonyms** you could use instead of the word 'big'.

tiny (large) gigantic   exciting   huge

pleasant   nasty   enormous

Try out some **synonyms** for the word 'nice' in this sentence.

This playground is _____.

Well done!

Comparative adjectives

When an **adjective** compares two nouns, it is called a **comparative adjective**.

My scarf is **long**.

Alf's scarf is **longer**.

Finish these sentences with the **comparative adjective**.

Jamie is fast.

Eliza is _____.

A bee is small.

A ladybird is _____.

Adjectives with three or more syllables (for example, 'a-maz-ing') use 'more' to make the **comparative** – e.g. **more** amazing

When an adjective compares three or more things, it is called a **superlative adjective**.

quick
└ adjective

quick**er**
└ comparative

quick**est**
└ superlative

Draw lines to link the adjectives to their **comparatives** and **superlatives**.

short	sadder	funniest
funny	softer	shortest
sad	funnier	saddest
soft	shorter	softest

Adjectives with three or more syllables (for example, 'beau-ti-ful') use 'most' to make the **superlative** – e.g. **most** beautiful

Well done!

Apostrophes · Contractions

An **apostrophe** can be used to show that letters are missing from a word or words. This is called a **contraction**.

does not ⟶ **doesn't**
she is ⟶ **she's**

Write down the **contractions** for these words.

can not _____

he will _____

I am _____

WATCH OUT FOR:

its it's   your you're

Try saying the sentences below out loud. If you can say 'it is' or 'you are', you need an apostrophe.

Tick which sentences have the **apostrophes** in the correct place.

Its sunny outside. ☐

You're going the wrong way. ☐

It's sunny outside. ☐

Your going the wrong way. ☐

An **apostrophe** can also show **possession** (that something belongs to someone).

The **cat's** purple pillow
William's lost shoe

Add an **apostrophe** to these sentences.

Melissas book is missing.

The girls coat is new.

The **apostrophe** goes **after** the 's' when the things belong to more than one person.

The **girls'** new footballs
The **dinosaurs'** spiky tails

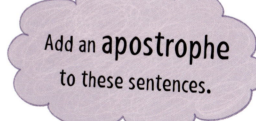

Add an **apostrophe** to these sentences.

The boys shirts are red.

The dogs tails are long.

Well done!

11

Conjunctions

Words and sentences can be joined together using **conjunctions** such as 'and', 'but', 'because'.

Underline the **conjunctions** in this email.

Dear Lizzie,

It was Sports Day today and I ran two races. I won the first one, but I fell over in the second race because Ursula tripped me up!

Join these sentences together by adding the **conjunction** 'and'. Remember to drop the full stop and change the capital letter.

My book is funny. It is a bit scary too.

A **main clause** is a group of words that includes a verb and that makes sense. A **subordinate clause** gives more meaning, but doesn't make sense on its own.

main clause

Megan couldn't finish her picture, because Tom wouldn't stay still.

subordinate clause

Underline the **subordinate clauses** in each of these sentences.

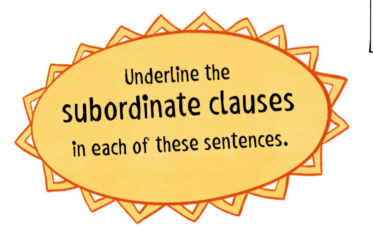

You can have a sandwich, if you're hungry.

Although he missed the bus, he arrived at school on time.

Well done!

13

Prepositions

A **preposition** shows how words in the sentence are related. It can describe positions, or when and how something happened.

The cat is **under** the bench.

preposition

The bird arrived **after** the cat.

preposition

Can you find all the **prepositions** in this word search?

in
under
off
on
beside
near
below
between

m a b e l o w
n o e s s n n
e f t i q u l
a f w c e n a
r b e s i d e
h l e i e e o
o n n n p r c